T0417746

# Deadly Quills

## Gross Porcupines

by Rex Ruby

BEARPORT
PUBLISHING

Minneapolis, Minnesota

**Credits**: Cover and title page, © s1pheeraphan/Getty Images and © Andrei Vasilev/iStock; Design elements throughout, © Andrei Vasilev/iStock; 5, © Michel & Christine Denis-Huot/Biosphoto; 6–7, © Sylvain Cordier/Biosphoto; 8–9, © miroslav_1/iStock; 10, © Custom Life Science Images/Alamy; 11, © Tobie Oosthuizen/Shutterstock; 12–13, © Linda Freshwaters Arndt/Alamy; 15, © pchoui/iStock; 16–17, © Tony Rix/Shutterstock; 17, © Kara Capaldo/iStock; 18–19, © Scenic Shutterbug/Shutterstock; and 20–21, © Debbie Steinhausser/Alamy.

**Bearport Publishing Company Product Development Team**
President: Jen Jenson; Director of Product Development: Spencer Brinker; Senior Editor: Allison Juda; Editor: Charly Haley; Associate Editor: Naomi Reich; Senior Designer: Colin O'Dea; Associate Designer: Elena Klinkner; Associate Designer: Kayla Eggert; Product Development Assistant: Anita Stasson

*Library of Congress Cataloging-in-Publication Data*

Names: Ruby, Rex, author.
Title: Deadly quills : gross porcupines / by Rex Ruby.
Description: Minneapolis, Minnesota : Bearport Publishing Company, [2023] | Series: Amazing animal self-defense | Includes bibliographical references and index.
Identifiers: LCCN 2022033640 (print) | LCCN 2022033641 (ebook) | ISBN 9798885093873 (library binding) | ISBN 9798885095099 (paperback) | ISBN 9798885096249 (ebook)
Subjects: LCSH: Porcupines--Juvenile literature. | Animal defenses--Juvenile literature.
Classification: LCC QL737.R652 R558 2023 (print) | LCC QL737.R652 (ebook) | DDC 599.35/97--dc23/eng/20220715
LC record available at https://lccn.loc.gov/2022033640
LC ebook record available at https://lccn.loc.gov/2022033641

For more information, write to Bearport Publishing, 5357 Penn Avenue South, Minneapolis, MN 55419.

# CONTENTS

# ARMED AND DANGEROUS

A hungry porcupine wanders around a field, looking for a snack. Then, out of nowhere, a lion appears. The scared porcupine raises its sharp **quills**. It swings its spiky tail and hits the lion . . . *ouch!* A bunch of quills stick into the big cat's face. The injured lion runs away.

A porcupine's **coat** is made of long hairs, soft fur, and about 30,000 **prickly** quills.

# BACK OFF!

A porcupine always warns its enemies before striking. First, the porcupine turns around and raises its needle-sharp quills. This shows off its longest, **stiffest** quills, which are found on the animal's back. If that doesn't work, the porcupine clicks its teeth together. This scary sound tells the enemy to leave before it gets hurt.

Another porcupine defense is to make a stinky smell. *Pee-yew!*

# A SPIKY TAIL

These warnings keep most animals away from a prickly porcupine. However, if an enemy comes too close after being warned, the porcupine attacks. The spiky little animal walks backward and slaps the enemy with its strong tail. Sharp quills stick into the enemy's skin.

Tail

Porcupines can lose several hundred quills in a single defensive attack.

# SHARP AND DEADLY

Getting struck by a porcupine's quills hurts! The tip of each quill has many tiny hooks that get lodged into the attacker's skin. This makes the sharp spikes hard to remove. If that's not bad enough, heat and moisture from the victim's body can pull the quills in even deeper. Sometimes, unlucky animals die if quills hit their heart or lungs.

A porcupine's skin has special protection, just in case the animal accidentally pokes itself!

# MANY ENEMIES

Most of a porcupine's enemies know not to mess with the prickly creature. Others learn the hard way. Still, there is one animal that can **outsmart** the porcupine. A **fisher** bites a porcupine's nose and flips it over. Then, the furry enemy attacks the porcupine's soft, quill-free belly.

A fisher

Wolves, coyotes, and owls are among the many animals that may try to attack a porcupine.

# HIGH AND LOW

There are about 23 kinds of porcupines that live around the world. Some live in forests. Their sharp **claws** help them climb trees. High up, they can sleep in safety. Others live in **grasslands** or deserts. They make their homes down low in **dens**. These may be in caves, old logs, or under piled rocks.

Porcupines are good swimmers! Their hollow quills help them float in the water.

# TASTY TREES

While only some kinds of porcupines climb trees, they all eat them! In fact, these little animals eat mostly trees during the winter. They use their long, orange teeth to bite off tough **bark**. These prickly creatures munch on the branches, leaves, and fruit, too.

Porcupines will sometimes eat small bugs or dead animals.

**Teeth**

17

# SOFT QUILLS

When it's time for babies, a mother porcupine heads to her den. She usually gives birth to only one baby at a time. The baby, called a porcupette, weighs about as much as two oranges. And it's born with a full set of tiny quills! Luckily for the mother, the quills are soft. They harden an hour or two later.

Some scientists think mother porcupines need extra salt. This may make them eat unusual foods, such as water plants—or even rubber mats!

# LIVING AND LEARNING

A porcupette drinks milk from its mother's body for up to four months. However, the baby can start searching for solid food a few weeks after it is born. Each night, the prickly porcupette follows its mother's grunts as they search for tasty meals. After about six months, the young porcupine is ready to live on its own.

A porcupine in the wild can live for up to 10 years.

# HEDGEHOG

Porcupines aren't the only animals with a prickly defense. The hedgehog has about 5,000 sharp spines that cover most of its body. When in danger, a hedgehog rolls its body into a tight ball. Only its spines show. The sharp points scare away most enemies.

**A hedgehog rolled into a ball**

# GLOSSARY

**bark** the tough covering on the outside of a tree

**claws** sharp nails at the tips of fingers or toes

**coat** thick fur or hair that covers some animals

**dens** homes where animals can rest, hide from enemies, and have babies

**fisher** a meat-eating mammal that lives in North America and is a member of the weasel family

**grasslands** dry areas covered with grass where only a few bushes and trees grow

**outsmart** to trick or beat by being more clever

**prickly** having small, sharp points

**quills** hard, sharp spines that make up part of a porcupine's coat

**stiffest** hardest to bend

23

# INDEX

## READ MORE

Sherman, Jill. *Porcupines (North American Animals).* Mankato, MN: Amicus, 2019.

Washburne, Sophie. *Porcupines in the Forest (Forest Creatures).* New York: Gareth Stevens, 2023.

Webster, Christine. *Porcupine (Backyard Animals).* New York: AV2, 2019.

## LEARN MORE ONLINE

1. Go to **www.factsurfer.com** or scan the QR code below.
2. Enter "**Deadly Quills**" into the search box.
3. Click on the cover of this book to see a list of websites.

## ABOUT THE AUTHOR

Rex Ruby lives in Minnesota with his family. He'd like to see a porcupine, but he doesn't want to get poked by its quills!